GARFIELD'S IRONCAT

Created by

JIM DAVIS

Written by Jim Kraft and Mark Acey
Designed and illustrated by Mike Fentz

Troll

This edition published in 2002 by Troll Communications L.L.C.
All rights reserved. No part of this book may be reproduced or utilized in any form or by
any means, electronic or mechanical, including photocopying, recording, or by any
information storage and retrieval system, without written permission from the publisher.
ISBN 0-8167-7431-5   Printed in the United States of America.
10 9 8 7 6 5 4 3 2 1

As the triathlon contestants were making the transition from biking to running, Jon Arbuckle was fighting to stay in the race. His lungs and legs ached. His feet slammed like bricks against the roadway. Still, he managed a smile as a short, fat runner rumbled past him, leaving a trail of sweat.

"That little fireplug seems to have sprung a leak," Jon joked to himself. Then he looked again. "Hey!" he cried. "That was no fireplug. That was my cat! Garfield, what are you doing in this triathlon?"

"Trying to survive it, what else?" gasped Garfield.

Of course, Garfield would never have competed in a triathlon in a million zillion years, if Jon hadn't entered the Mona Kona Ironman Triathlon in Hawaii; and if Jon hadn't been forced to take Garfield along, because the kennel said they would rather keep a rabid wolverine than baby-sit Garfield again; and if the first prize weren't something very, *VERY* special.

The prize was a symbolic "key to the islands," which meant that for a whole week the winner could go anywhere and do anything on the islands—for *free!*

It's almost as good as getting a wish from a genie, thought Garfield. *Except then I could wish all dogs to Siberia. Still, this is the next best thing—and I know just what I'll do when I win!*

Naturally, Garfield hadn't bothered to train for the race.

How tough can a triathlon be? he thought. *If Jon can do it, anyone with half a muscle can.* Garfield poked at his pudgy body. *I must have half a muscle here somewhere.*

So that's how Garfield found himself leaping into the water for the first leg of the Mona Kona Ironman Triathlon: a 2.4-mile swim across Mona Kona Bay. There was just one little problem: Garfield was a terrible swimmer. But he wasn't about to let that stop him. While Jon and the other competitors plowed through the waves, Garfield bobbed lazily on his inner tube, which he had equipped with an outboard motor!—and, of course, a picnic lunch.

Brains beat brawn every time, he thought, smiling.

Garfield gazed contentedly at the water.

"This is my idea of gruelling competition," he said. "A little sun . . . a cool drink . . . a big sandwich . . . a monster shark . . . A MONSTER SHARK!"

Garfield flipped into the ocean as the inner tube exploded between the shark's giant jaws.

In seconds Garfield was speeding through the water like a furry torpedo.

"Out of my way! Out of my way!" he shouted to the other swimmers. "Sharkbait coming through!" The fat cat swam at panic speed until he ran aground on the beach.

SKIP!

SKIP!

"Fear is a great motivator," he said as he stood up slowly and knocked the sand out of his ears. "Okay, I survived part one. Now all I need to do is get on my bicycle and pedal for . . . 112 miles?! Are they crazy? I can't do it! My posterior will be paralyzed for life!"

But Garfield desperately wanted the key to the islands, and his greed was even stronger than his will to whine. Grumbling, he climbed onto his bicycle and rolled back into the race.

The first part of the bike race followed a steep and winding course up the slope of Mt. Mona Kona, an ancient, but active, volcano. Garfield was soon in trouble.

"I can't go on," he gasped. "My legs feel mushier than Odie's brain."

But then Garfield noticed Jon riding just ahead of him. Reaching out, Garfield secretly slipped a claw through Jon's shirttail. Unaware that he was now towing a flabby trailer, Jon strained against the pedals of his bike.

"If only I can get to the top of the mountain," Jon grunted.

"I'd help," said Garfield, "but I didn't bring my whip."

With tremendous effort, Jon reached the summit at last. There the trail took a sharp turn. Jon's shirttail ripped away.

"I feel a crash coming on," said Garfield, as he bounced off the road and over the lip of the volcano!

Garfield bumped and skidded down the inside of the crater,
finally landing in the mouth of the volcano, where he stuck like a cork.
"Help! Get me out!" Garfield cried. "I don't look good in lava!"

BURRRP!

With Garfield blocking the volcano's mouth, there was no way for the hot gases to escape. Pressure began to build inside the mountain. The crater started to tremble. Then, with a great roar, Mt. Mona Kona belched Garfield out of the volcano! Several miles and a thousand screams later, he landed in a palm tree . . . just across the finish line of the bike race.

"I did it," mumbled Garfield. "I survived the second leg. All I have to do now is . . . *run 26 miles*?! No way! This violates all the laws of laziness! I demand an investigation! I demand a lawyer! I demand directions to the nearest luau!"

Nevertheless, Garfield did get back in the race. And it was torture. Sweat poured from him like the drool from Odie's mouth. His heart was exploding like the turkey Jon cooked last Thanksgiving. His tail was dragging like a day with Nermal. And that was all in the first twenty yards!

"I want to lie down, I want to lie down," Garfield muttered to himself. "I want first prize. But mostly I want to lie down!"

Garfield struggled for a few more miles, then collapsed.

"That's it," he wheezed. "I'm wiped out. I'm through. The sweat stops here."

As Garfield sprawled on the pavement, several runners passed him by, including a 102-year-old sailor with a peg leg, a sweaty sumo wrestler—and Jon, who was now crawling on all fours.

"Something tells me I'm not in the lead," said Garfield.

Garfield's chances of winning the race were about the same as Jon's chances of dating a supermodel. But just when all looked lost, the exhausted cat heard a noise behind him. Turning around, he saw a boy riding toward him on a skateboard. Though Garfield's body was stalled, his brain immediately shifted into overdrive.

"It's fate," said Garfield, scrambling to his feet. "Here comes my ticket to victory!"

As the boy passed him, Garfield made his move.

"Excuse me, sonny," said the fat cat as he bumped the boy from the skateboard. "I'm borrowing this for a good cause— 'cause I need it!"

Garfield pushed off with his foot and raced away.

"Let the good times roll! Next stop . . . the finish line!"

BUMP!

Just then the road took a sudden slope downward. Within moments, Garfield started to go faster . . . and faster . . . and faster!

"Yee-ha!" he yelled. "I'm built for speed!" And indeed, his great weight was causing him to accelerate down the hill. The fat cat was soon an orange blur, streaking past—and through—the runners ahead of him.

"Outta my way, slowpokes!" he cried. "I'm 'Lord of the Board' and I rule the road!"

On Garfield zoomed, mile after mile, passing runner after runner, till at last he spied the finish line far in the distance. Unfortunately, a few runners were already nearing the line.

"It's hopeless," said Garfield. "I'll never catch them. It's impossib—"

KLONK! Suddenly Garfield's skateboard smacked into a tortoise crossing the road! The impact instantly sent Garfield rocketing through the air.

Seconds later, he landed behind the runners and, like a burly bowling ball, bashed into them, toppling them like bowling pins. Garfield rolled across the finish line and finally came to a stop at the judge's feet.

"Ladies and gentlemen," announced the judge, "we have our winner." The judge helped the fatigued feline to his feet, then presented him with the grand prize, the key to the islands. The crowd cheered as Garfield hoisted the large plastic key over his head.

"Do you have anything to say?" the judge asked.

"Yeah, alert all the islands' pizza parlors," replied the cat, rubbing his growling tummy. "Hurricane Garfield is on the way!"